Sylvia Karavis and Gill Matthews

Have Your SAY

Acknowledgements

Photos

Keith Lillis, cover, title page (except far right), contents page top, page 15 and index. Gareth Boden, title page far right, contents page bottom, pages 4–9, 11–13, 15, 18 and 19. Roger Scruton, page 10. Robert E. Daemmrich/Tony Stone Images, page 16. Sally and Richard Greenhill, pages 17, 21 main and 23 main. Ace Photo library, pages 20 and 22.

Illustrations

Barry Atkinson, page 14. All other illustrations by Oxford Illustrators and M2.

Thanks

Many thanks to Whaddon Primary School and Gordonbrock Primary School.

Heinemann Educational Publishers
Halley Court, Jordan Hill, Oxford OX2 8EJ
a division of Reed Educational & Professional Publishing Limited

Heinemann is a registered trademark of Reed Educational & Professional Publishing Limited

OXFORD MELBOURNE AUCKLAND
JOHANNESBURG BLANTYRE GABORONE
IBADAN PORTSMOUTH (NH) USA CHICAGO

© Sylvia Karavis and Gill Matthews, 1998

The moral right of the proprietors has been asserted.

First published 1998

05

10 9

British Library Cataloguing in Publication Data
A catalogue record for this book is available from the British Library.

ISBN 0 435 09661 3   *Have Your Say* single copy
ISBN 0 435 09662 1   *Have Your Say* 6 copy pack

Designed by M2
Printed and bound in China by China Translation & Printing Services Ltd.

Contents

Introduction

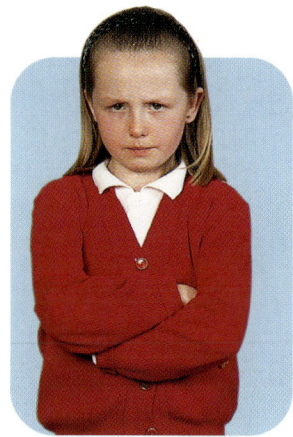

Children and adults often discuss issues that matter to them. These issues range from those that may be sorted out at home and at school to others of wider interest that are difficult for small groups of people to resolve.

In this book, some children, teachers and parents from Whaddon Primary School in Cheltenham have expressed their views on issues that interest them. This book is about their different points of view. In some cases both sides of the argument are presented; in others you are given only one side.

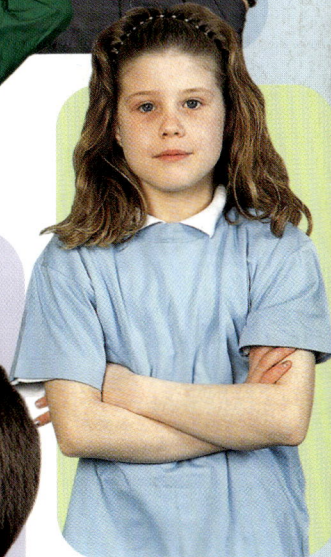

You can use this book to begin discussions and to help you to think about how to present an argument. How do you feel about these issues?

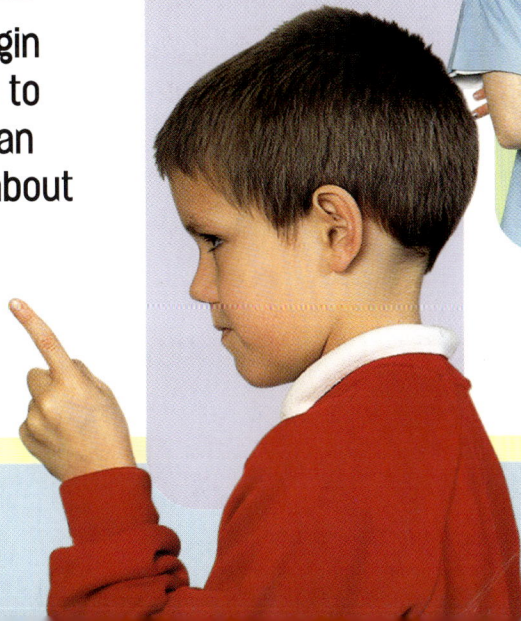

5

FOOTBALL IN THE PLAYGROUND

WHOSE SIDE ARE YOU ON?

At Whaddon Primary School, some children play football in the playground at breaktime. Other children are getting fed up of their playground being used as a football pitch. Here children, teachers and parents give opinions for and against being allowed to play football in the playground.

FOR

- 'Children should be able to enjoy football in an informal, social way.'

- 'We should have ball games because both girls and boys love them.'

- 'Playing football teaches children to co-operate.'

- 'Football lets children use their energy and is good exercise.'

- 'Playing football wakes children up in the morning and makes them lively.'

- 'Children can practise and become professional.'

- 'What is the point of learning football if you can't play it in the playground?'

Children in Years 3 to 6 were asked whether they would like to see football banned in the playground at breaktime. This chart shows the number in favour of banning. ↓

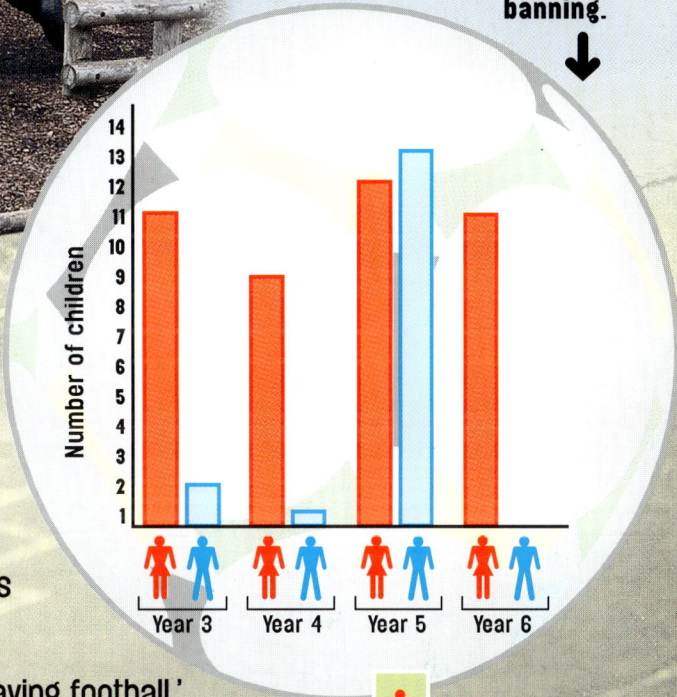

Number of children

Year 3   Year 4   Year 5   Year 6

Girls
Boys

AGAINST

❌ 'Football should only be played in one area so non-football players have space to play.'

❌ 'You can't get past the children playing football.'

❌ 'Little children are in danger of being hurt. Even small children can kick the ball hard.'

❌ 'Football causes arguments and fights.'

❌ 'My sons are ruining their shoes and trousers.'

❌ 'Footballs can smash windows'.

❌ 'Football should be banned because people are horrible to you when they play.'

At breaktime, will you be on the pitch or on the playground?

Homework or home play?

Teachers and politicians have recently been discussing how much homework children should be given. Some people think children should have more homework because it helps them to do better at school. Others think that children should be free to play after school. How much homework do you think you should have?

Children think...

'You might be tired after working hard at school, so you might just want to watch television.'

'It's good to have homework instead of watching TV.'

'I have to go to Brownies and other places so I don't have much time.'

'You need to think for yourself so you can learn.'

'You might be tired, so you won't be able to think clearly.'

'We have to get used to homework because we will have it in secondary school.'

Chris Davis, chairman of the National Association for Primary Education, said: 'Children do need time to switch off as well, but most of us agree they spend far too much time in front of the television.'

Source: *The Times*, 28 October 1995

Parents think...

'Children should have time for play and imagination.'

'They have enough work to do at school.'

'Homework teaches children routine.'

'They have too much time on their hands.'

'Children's leisure time should be for playing.'

Teachers think...

'Any form of homework is an important part of learning.'

'Children enjoy sharing school activities.... and it gives parents a chance to show that they value school work.'

'Homework teaches good study habits.'

'Some children have after school activities so they do not have a lot of spare time in the evenings.'

Primary school children spend an hour a week on homework, compared with two-and-a-half hours every night watching television. Pupils in Japan and many European countries spend 50% longer on work at home than British schoolchildren.

Source: *The Times*, 28 October 1995

This chart shows the average number of hours per day that children in the last year of primary school spend on doing their homework.

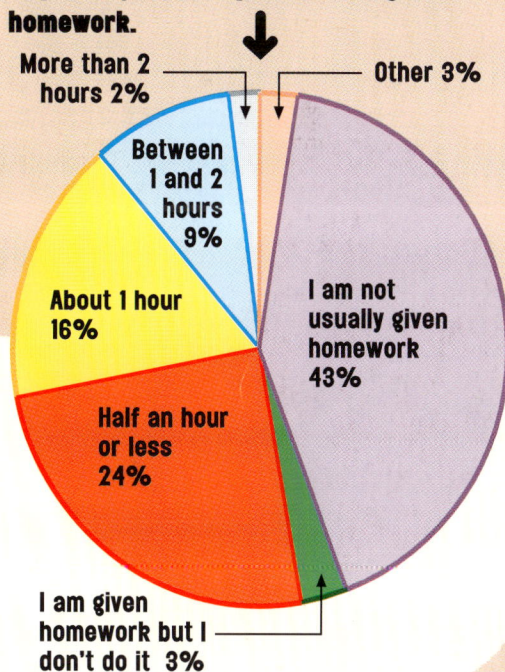

More than 2 hours 2%

Other 3%

Between 1 and 2 hours 9%

About 1 hour 16%

I am not usually given homework 43%

Half an hour or less 24%

I am given homework but I don't do it 3%

Source: *Excellence in Schools*, Department for Education and Employment, HMSO, London, April 1998

Switch off that television!

Do you think you should be able to watch television wherever and whenever you want? People often worry about the amount of TV children watch. If they watch too much TV, children might not do other things like homework or exercise. If children are allowed to watch whatever they want, they might watch programmes which are not suitable for them.

Children and parents at the school were asked whether they think children should be allowed to watch TV in their bedrooms. Here are some of their opinions.

This chart shows the average number of hours per day that children in the last year of primary school spend watching television and videos. ➡

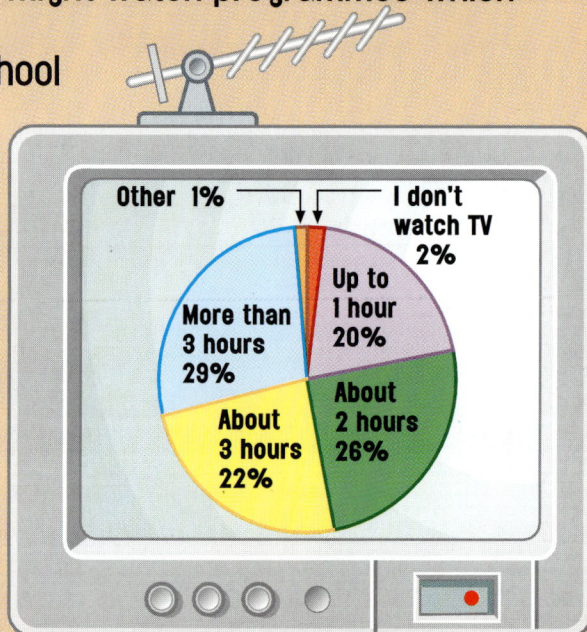

Other 1%
I don't watch TV 2%
Up to 1 hour 20%
About 2 hours 26%
About 3 hours 22%
More than 3 hours 29%

Source: *Excellence in Schools*, Department for Education and Employment, HMSO, London, April 1998

'My children have televisions in their bedrooms because I think it helps them to unwind. It is important to let children choose what they want to watch, although I do check on them. Since they have had TVs in their rooms we have not argued as much about what to watch. I get to watch the soaps I want to watch!'

'I don't think so because children copy what they see and hear, like bad language. Also, it costs more to have two televisions on in the house. There's also safety to consider. Children might fall asleep with the TV on and there could be a fire.'

'No, I don't. The bedroom is a place of rest and relaxation, not violence and noise. What's more, if children have TVs in their bedrooms there is a great temptation to stay awake far too late.'

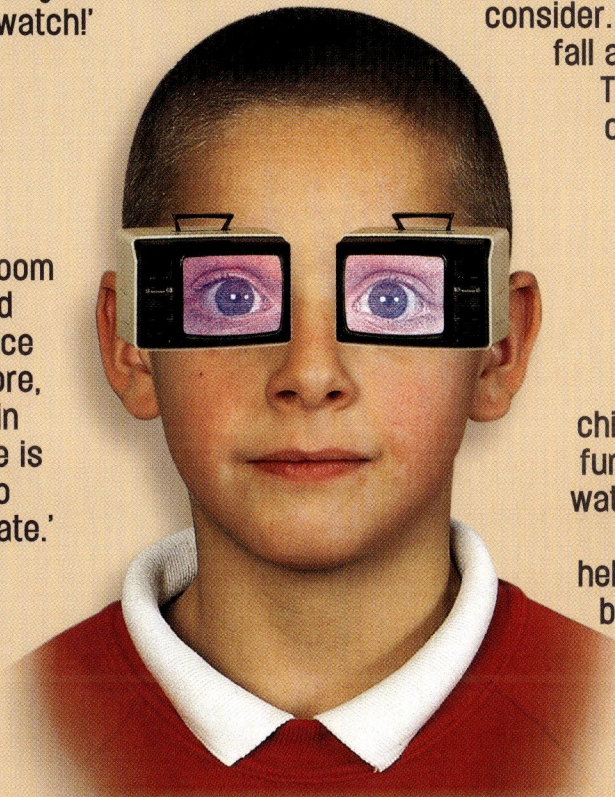

'Yes, I do. It keeps children quiet and it's fun to watch TV. I like watching my favourite programmes and it helps me settle down before I go to sleep. Most of all it gives me time to be on my own.'

People have different views about this issue. What do you think? Would you think differently if you were a parent?

The great pocket money debate

Children and their parents often disagree about pocket money. You might think that you can be trusted to spend your pocket money sensibly, but your parents might think differently!

On these two pages, some children and parents discuss whether or not they agree with the following opinion: 'Pocket money gives children a sense of responsibility and makes them aware of the value of money.'

Agree...

Children...

...can save up for presents and holidays

...are taught about maths in real situations

...should be given money so that they have some independence

...will not envy others if they have money of their own

...can buy the things they like

...have the choice to support causes they are interested in

Disagree...

Children...

...will spend it all at once

...might lose money when they are out

...need to learn that money has to be earned

...might be bullied or have their pocket money stolen from them

...cannot be trusted to spend it wisely

...will become greedy and keep wanting more

The value of money changes over time. A child with £5 in 1975 could buy much more than a child with the same amount in 1995. ⬇

	1975	1985	1995	2005
Large chocolate bar	31p	84p	£1.07	?
T-Shirt	£1.00	£2.99	£7.00	?
Single record or CD	65p	£1.55	£2.29	?
Book	90p	£1.50	£3.99	?
Cinema ticket	£1.49	£1.97	£3.55	?

Sources: Cadburys, Marks and Spencer, HMV, UBIS, British Film Council

Do you think children should have pocket money? If so, how much should they have?

Can you handle your health?

Do you want good health, long life, energy, strong teeth and bones, to fight infection and to grow? Yes? On this page are some facts about eating the right foods to stay healthy. On the next page, some children give their opinions on eating healthy food.

The health food facts

A healthy body needs the right sorts of food. You need protein for body building, carbohydrates and fat for energy, and vitamins and minerals for protection and general good health.

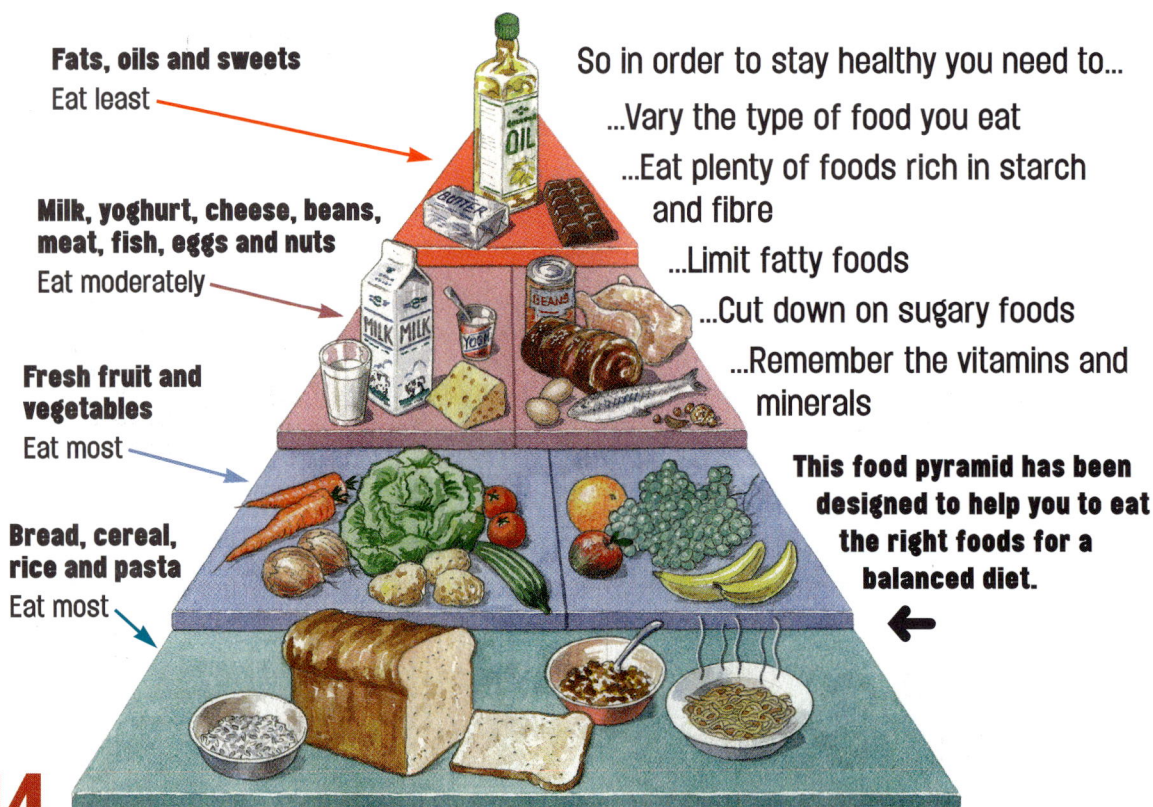

Fats, oils and sweets
Eat least

Milk, yoghurt, cheese, beans, meat, fish, eggs and nuts
Eat moderately

Fresh fruit and vegetables
Eat most

Bread, cereal, rice and pasta
Eat most

So in order to stay healthy you need to...

...Vary the type of food you eat

...Eat plenty of foods rich in starch and fibre

...Limit fatty foods

...Cut down on sugary foods

...Remember the vitamins and minerals

This food pyramid has been designed to help you to eat the right foods for a balanced diet.

←

14

Source: Health Education Authority

What they say

If you eat lots of fatty food and sugar your skin will feel horrible and dull and you will get spots.

I like eating chips. I eat them every day. Anyway, we need fat to keep us warm, so I always choose chips.

If you don't eat healthy food your teeth will go bad

If I can't choose I won't eat and then I'll get ill.

Sugar gives us energy.

You've read the facts and the opinions... your health is in your hands.

Calling all sleepyheads...

Can I just stay up to watch this TV programme?

I just want to finish the book I'm reading.

How often have you come up with excuses like these to avoid going to bed? Maybe the following will convince you that you need your sleep...

Sleep is important. Nobody fully understands why we need sleep, but scientists think that the body uses the time to recover and to repair damage. When we fall asleep our heart and breathing rates slow down, muscles relax and our senses rest. If this is the case, are you giving your body enough rest?

Lack of sleep means that the body and the brain do not work properly. If you don't go to bed at a reasonable time, you will be sleepy in class and not learn as much. Tiredness means you may not be able to think clearly, and you may also be a danger to other people. Accidents can happen. You will lack energy, and even playing becomes too much of an effort. Is staying up late really worth it?

There is some truth in the old saying 'Early to bed and early to rise, makes us healthy, wealthy and wise.' Next time you start to argue about your bedtime, remember your body needs a break. Give it a rest.

It's not late yet...

But you're not going to bed yet, Dad. Why should I have to?

It's not fair! I'm not tired!

Children at Whaddon Primary School were asked what time they usually go to bed.

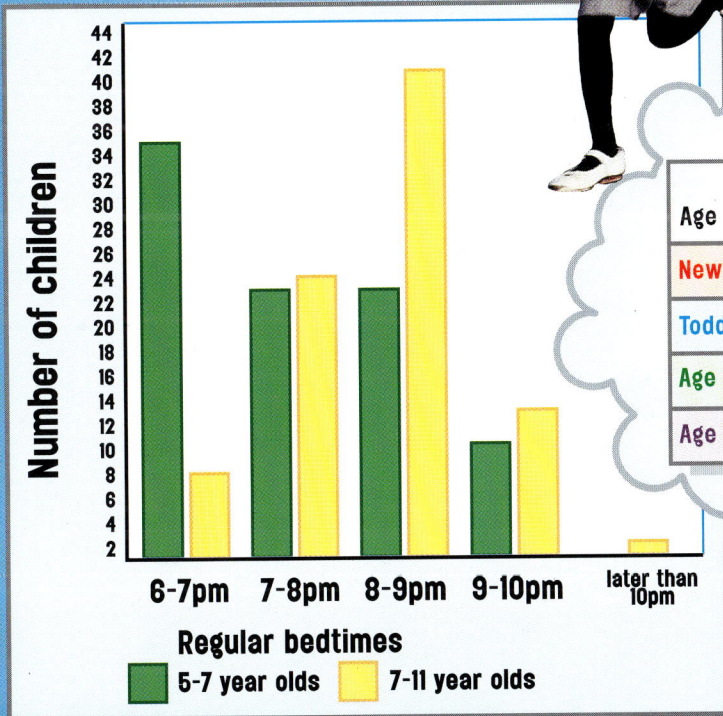

Chart: Number of children vs Regular bedtimes

Y-axis: Number of children (2 to 44)

X-axis: Regular bedtimes — 6-7pm, 7-8pm, 8-9pm, 9-10pm, later than 10pm

Legend: 5-7 year olds (green), 7-11 year olds (yellow)

Age	Number of hours of sleep needed each night
Newborn	Up to 16
Toddler	12
Age 3–5	10–12
Age 5–11	10

This chart shows how many hours of sleep children need each night.

Source: Sleep Products Safety Council

17

The pros and cons of school uniform

How do you feel about school uniforms? Do you think they look smart, or are you happier wearing your own clothes? Here is a look at both sides of the argument.

Many schools have a rule that children wear school uniform. Other schools have no rules about uniforms. Some children and parents are quite happy to follow these rules. Others, however, feel that children should not have to wear a uniform.

Wearing school uniform means that everybody looks and feels the same so nobody looks smarter or more fashionable than anybody else. It encourages a feeling of belonging and being part of a larger group, therefore children become proud of their school.

Uniforms tend to be practical and hard-wearing because they are designed to stand up to the wear and tear of school life. In addition, wearing a uniform means that other clothes are not worn out at school. Finally, having to wear a school uniform prevents children from asking for fashionable clothes and expensive designer labels in order to keep up with their friends.

> It saves me having to decide what to wear each day.

> Uniforms make you look bright and clever.

> When people come to visit the school they are impressed.

18

We may want to show our other clothes off.

Teachers don't wear uniforms so why should we?

Uniforms are either too hot or too cold.

On the other hand, children cannot show that they are individuals if they are all dressed alike. They need to have the chance to develop their own likes and dislikes. Not everybody feels comfortable in the styles and colours of uniforms.

Children grow quickly, so wearing a uniform means that they don't get the wear out of their ordinary clothes. Having to buy a uniform could be seen as a waste of money. Most of all, children are keen to follow fashion trends, and uniforms tend not to be fashionable.

In conclusion, there are many reasons both for and against wearing school uniform. Whatever is decided, it is important that children's clothing is practical and that every child feels comfortable with what they are wearing.

Should traffic be banned from city centres?

The amount of traffic in towns and cities is increasing. This is causing more accidents and more pollution. Many towns and cities are introducing traffic-free zones to try to reduce the amount of traffic. Pedestrians and cycles are allowed into these areas, but cars and lorries are banned. Some people think that these zones are a good idea, but other people think that they are not the right way to solve the traffic problem.

The next four pages of this book look at this issue. On pages 20 and 21 you will find an argument in favour of traffic-free zones. On pages 22 and 23 you will find an argument against traffic-free zones. Both arguments are supported by facts and opinions from people directly affected by pedestrianisation.

In favour of traffic-free zones

In this age of the motor car, traffic-free zones are important if we are to make life pleasant for everybody.

People need to feel safe in their environment, be able to move about, visit friends and play without worrying about the hazard of busy roads. Fast-moving traffic is a danger to pedestrians, particularly children and the elderly. Not only do many accidents happen where children play near roads, but also elderly people find it difficult to cross the road quickly and safely.

OPINION: I like playing outside, but it's too dangerous outside my house because of all the cars.

David Smith, 8

Scientists have analysed exhaust fumes and have found that they add to pollution. Pollution can make it difficult for some people to breathe; others become ill. In addition, traffic noise makes it difficult to hear and talk.

Traffic-free zones are areas where trees and flowers can be planted. In crowded towns and cities they become places where people can meet, talk and relax. Traffic-free zones encourage people to walk or cycle to work and school, which helps them to stay fit.

FACT: Children who live within 500m of busy roads are 30% more likely to be admitted to hospital with asthma than those who live further away.

Source: Sarah Walters, Birmingham University research paper, 1997

OPINION: My shop has been much busier since they pedestrianised the city centre. It's a much more pleasant environment for people to shop in.

Jane McWilliams, bookshop manager

For everybody's health and safety, people and traffic should be kept apart.

FACT: 9 out of 10 children own a bicycle but less than 1% use it to get to school.

Source: Cycle Touring and Campaigning, October/November 1995

Should traffic be banned from city centres?

Against traffic-free zones

Traffic-free zones would make life very inconvenient for families with young children, and for elderly and disabled people.

People need to have the freedom to come and go as they please. They should be able to park near their homes rather than having to walk, which could be both dangerous and frightening, particularly at night. Elderly people often find it difficult to walk any distance without getting tired. Even buses would not be able to stop within easy reach of housing, which means that many people would find it difficult to go shopping, get to work or school or visit friends. Vehicles would not be able to make deliveries, and services such as repair vans would not be able to visit.

FACT: Surveys show that most shop owners are worried about pedestrianisation. Shop owners are concerned that people will travel to out-of-town shopping centres rather than shop in the city centre.

Source: Oxfordshire County Council, 1998

OPINION: Since they pedestrianised my street, buses don't stop outside my house any more. I can't walk very far, so I don't go out much any more.

Florence Johnson, 76

In any case, it is impossible to completely pedestrianise an area, as emergency vehicles need to be able to reach fires and people needing medical help.

For everybody's convenience, people should be able to travel wherever and whenever they wish.

Index